PLEASANT PETS

ADULT COLORING BOOK

PRAISE MY PET!

WWW.PRAISEMYPET.COM

Color Buster!

Color Pete Jingles!

3

Color Brownie!

Color Meredith Grey!

Color Oscar and Benji!

18

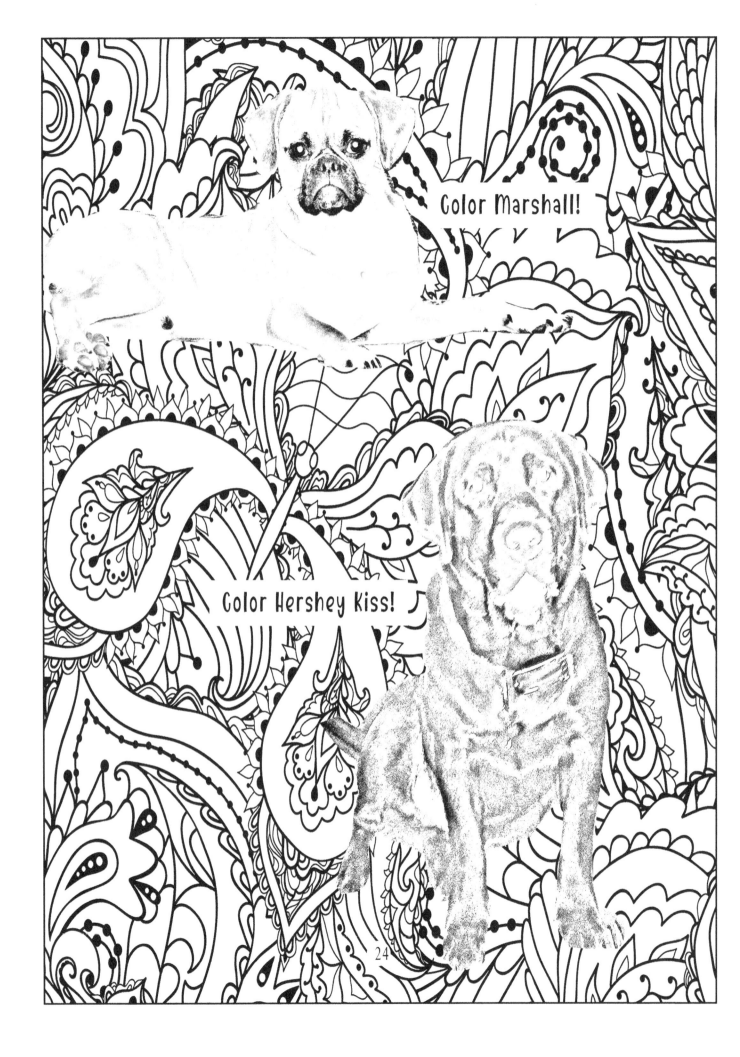

Color Jasper!

Color Chet!

25

Color Ziggy!

Color Chloe!

29

Color Bonnie, Clyde and Cooper!

Color Jaxon and Rico!

32

Color LaLa ArmiJo!

Color Zen!

Color Bazinga!

38

Color Brady Puppa Head Hulme!

Color Jay!

Color Sadie Mae!

Color Button, Monty and Treacle!

46

Color Zephyr!

Color Dante and Daisy!

Color Buddy!

Color Jazz!

60

Color Elvis and Chloe!

62

Color Petey!

Color Covid!

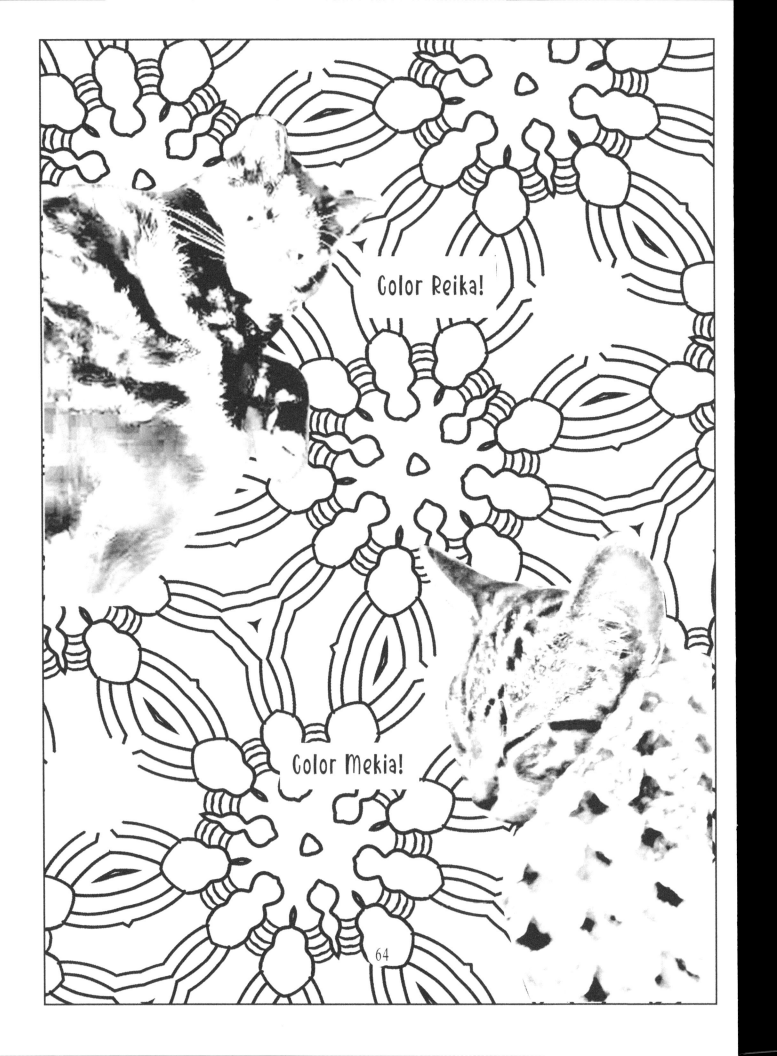

Color Davina!

Color Tombstone!

72

Color Sushi and Coco!

Color Frankie and Harley!

75

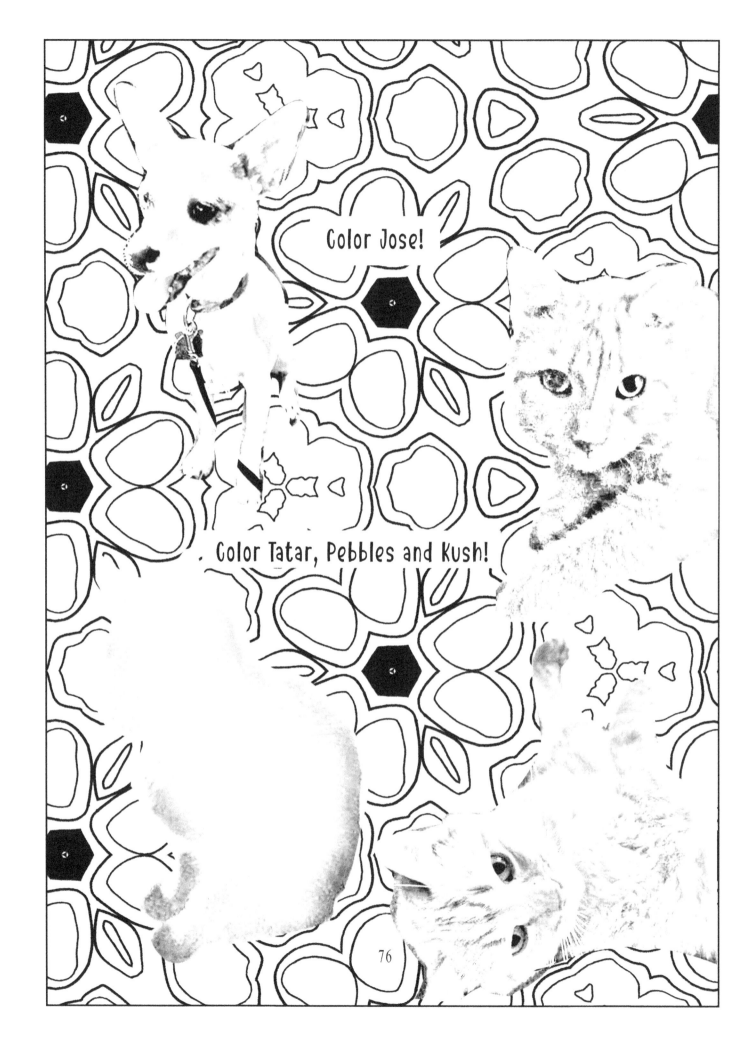

76

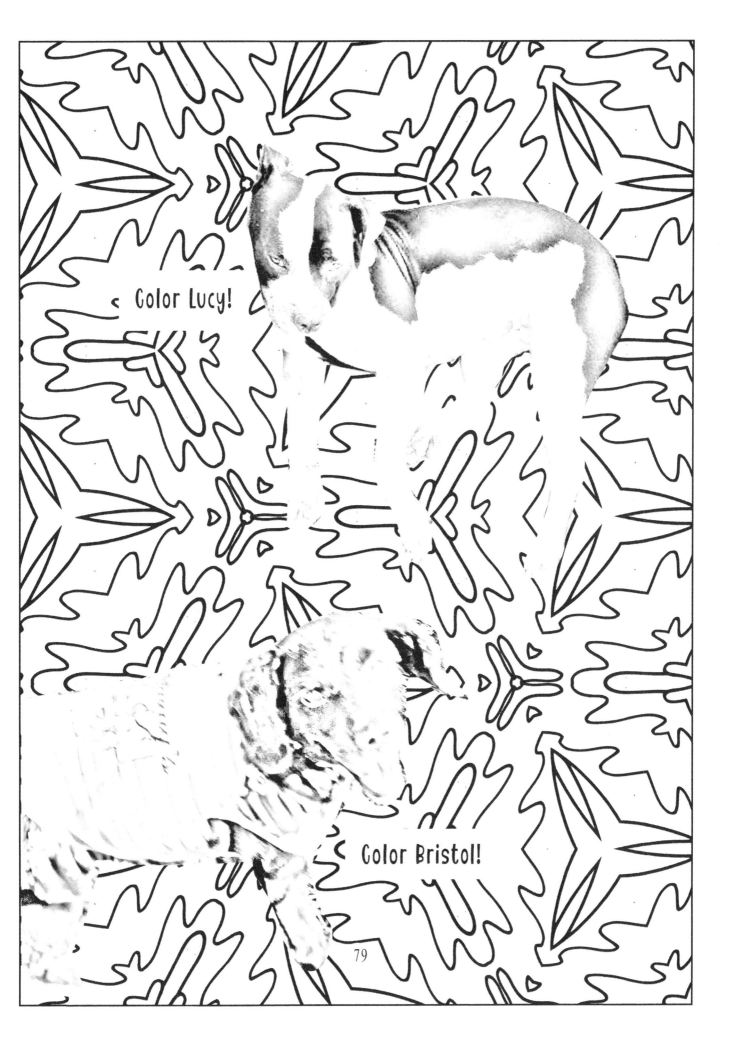

Color Lucy!

Color Bristol!

79

Color Remy and Bronson!

82

Color Christine Parker!

Color Rosie!

84

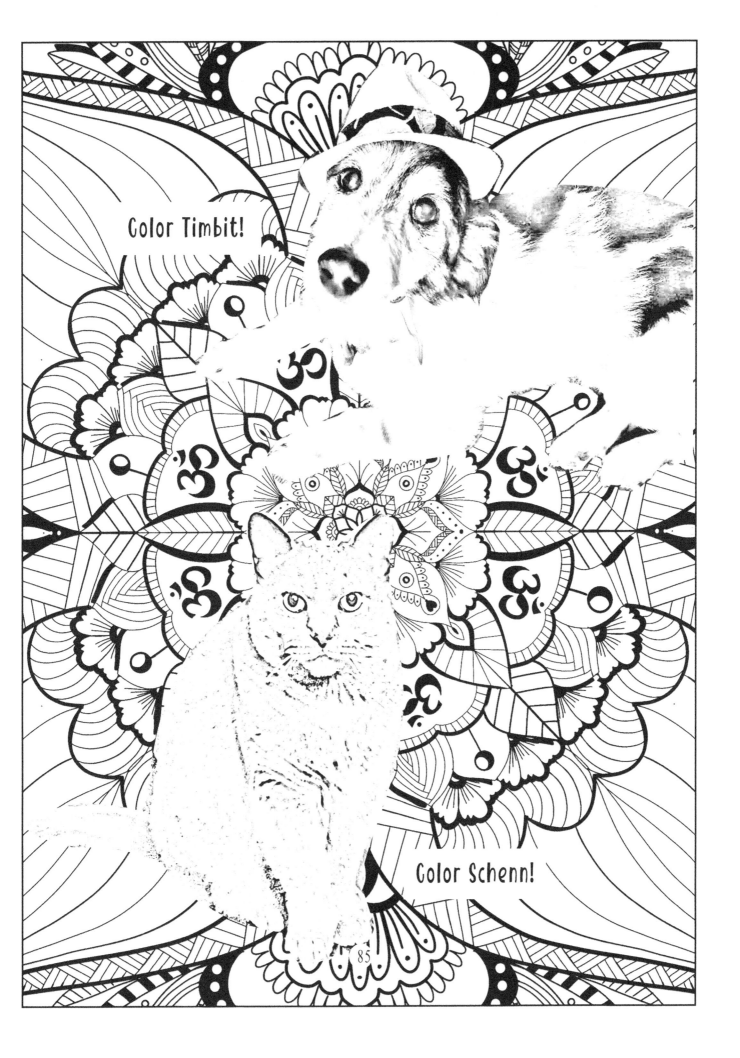

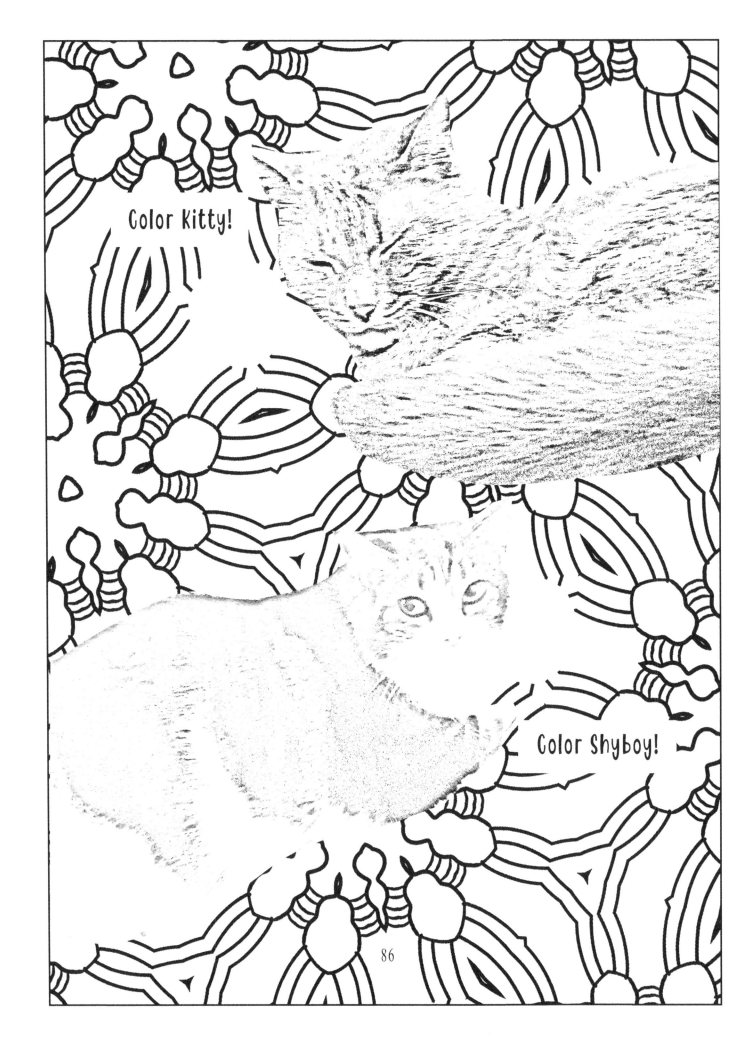

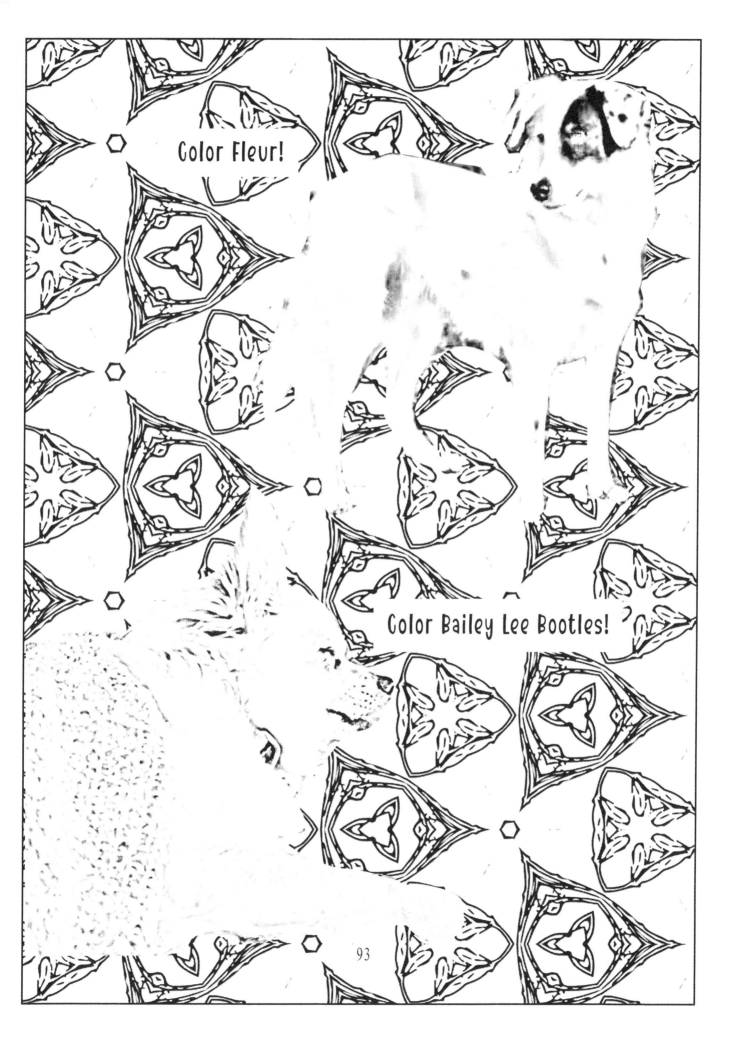

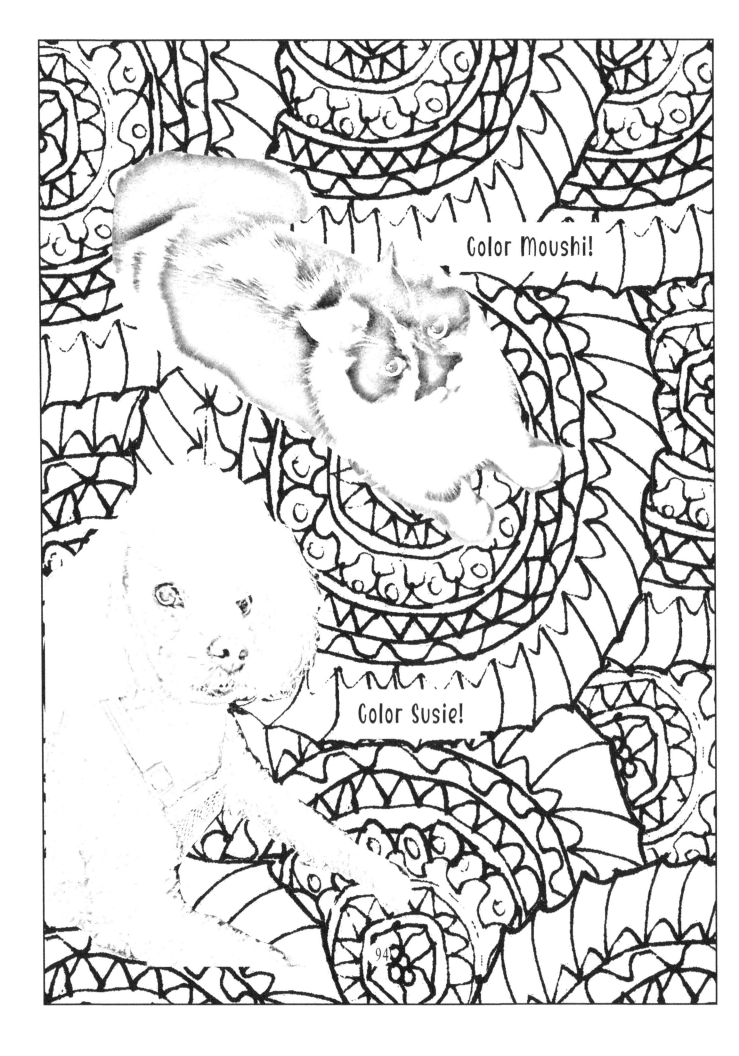

Color Jackson, Lily and Gemma!

95

Color Millie and Griffin!

Color Toki Loki and Boogie Woogie!

Color Marvin!

100

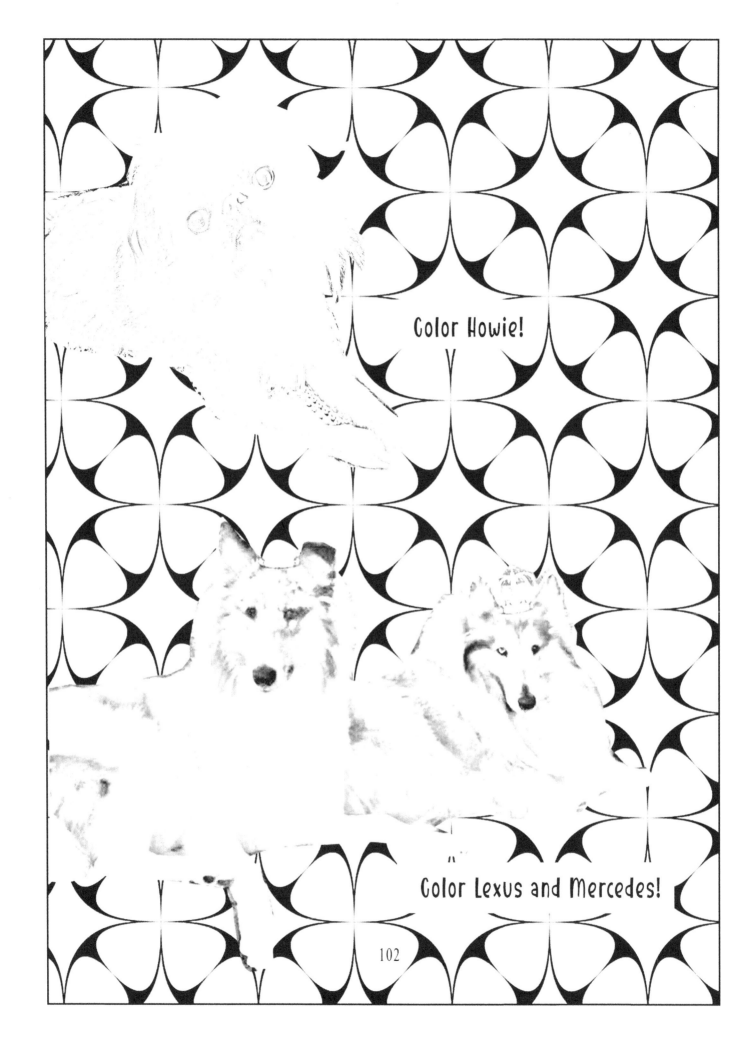

Color Howie!

Color Lexus and Mercedes!

We hope you enjoyed our coloring book! If you'd like to see YOUR pet in one of our upcoming coloring books, visit www.praisemypet.com/pages/send-us-your-pet-photos

Happy coloring!

Made in the USA
Monee, IL
17 December 2020